Snapshot in the Dark

Stephen Smithyman

Snapshot in the Dark
& other poems 1976–2012

For Joy, Mia and Pablo

Snapshot in the Dark
ISBN 978 1 76041 588 4
Copyright © text Stephen Smithyman 2018

First published 2018 by
GINNINDERRA PRESS
PO Box 3461 Port Adelaide 5015 Australia
www.ginninderrapress.com.au

Contents

Gone Fishing	7
Snapshot in the Dark	8
Summer in Central Otago	10
With My Father At Te Kopuru	11
At My Mother's Funeral	12
Last Day With My Brother	13
The Smell of Coffee	15
Memories of Nile Road and Wairau Creek	16
Learning to Fall	18
Bowling Green	19
Waiting for the Penguins	20
Plenty	23
The Road to the Coast	25
The Market	27
Six Poems Based on Paintings by Edward Hopper	28
Swimming in the Mediterranean	35
Interior at Petworth	37
A Walk on Hampstead Heath	38
At Haworth	39
At Castle Howard	41
Cutting the Grass	42
Briagolong Sundays	43
Wattle in Winter	44
A Perfect Night For Shooting Stars	45
The World is a Garden	47
Briagolong Mornings	49
The Last of the Season	50
Black Snake on the Road	51
Goanna in the Grass	53
Four Birds	55

Hare	56
Giant Swing	57
That Valley, That Shadow	60
Interrupted Journeys	61
Mother's Day	63
Wet Winter	64
Washington Square Blues	65
At the Hotel Chelsea	66
Wall Street	67
Brooklyn Bridge	68
Storm in Boston	70
Return to Melbourne	72
In Praise of Nectarines	74
In Memory of George Haydn, 1919–2005	75
An Old Dog's Tale	76

Gone Fishing

We were sitting up in bed.
I was eating bread
and you were writing poems.
Behind us was an open window –
glimpses of the bay,
nearly full tide, a beach,
a hillside covered with manuka,
mangroves at the base, clouds
at the summit, the sky –
and all reflected
in an oval wardrobe mirror,
dim with the years, dusty
with disuse, like one of those
murky sepia prints, framed
in cardboard, of our parents
on a fishing expedition in 1932,
posed on the running board
of a Model A Ford,
just before setting out, knees up,
chests out, smiling vaguely
towards the camera, dazzled
by sunlight, so proud of the catch
they obviously already had in mind.

Snapshot in the Dark

Here you are, standing
in the doorway, looking
like a little child.
It is like someone
just turned a light on you
and everything else is dark.
It is a Victorian veranda
in full daylight, hard-edged,
extreme. The light
cuts across the veranda
and falls on you.
Everything else is dark.
You are wearing
the expression of a child,
bright-eyed, mischievous.
A print frock, of some fabric
filmy, delicate, clings
to your body and legs.
You are wearing
the expression of a child.
You are saying something,
waving goodbye.
I am walking
down a path, through
an overgrown garden.

When I close my eyes,
I can see you now.
It is like the moment after
looking at the sun,
the bright spot dancing
in front of the eyes,
like a bright spot dancing
in my memory, like taking
a snapshot of you in the dark.

Summer in Central Otago

A landscape like the surface of the moon –
grey pitted rock with very little vegetation,
except for wild thyme, growing low down
between the rocks, the smell rising in the wind –
working all day in the orchard, drinking
at night with the backpackers in the local hotel…
One day, I was so hungover, I couldn't distinguish
any direction. I had to sit at the bottom
of my ladder until my head stopped spinning.
All I could see was rows, rows, rows…
On Sundays, we would climb the hills
above the orchard to the dam, where we
dived from the dam wall, caught yabbies,
picked field mushrooms big as dinner plates,
stole corn from the neighbouring farmer's patch,
took the lot back and cooked it up
on the single hotplate in the pickers' hut…
                                On days
when it was too hot to work, we would stand
on the hill above the orchard, looking out
across the valley floor, the ice-green
of the Clutha and the darker green of
the orchards clustered along its banks
making a cool contrast with that parched
desert brown, to where the distant Remarkables
hung in space, at the limits of our perception,
snow-capped in the shimmering summer heat.

With My Father At Te Kopuru

A man may connect thus with his origins:
it is a form of musing, like falling asleep.
We stood at the gateposts, on the edge
of the overgrown paddock, in the warmth
of the afternoon sun. The gateposts
were all that remained of the Old Men's Home
where my father spent his childhood.
The paddock ended in willows and a creek.
A cold wind blew, chasing the clouds across,
and we woke from his dream of a life
so long ago – the dead men, the crippled heroes,
his mother and father fighting and making love.
Somewhere, elsewhere, that creek ran on
and, where it came out, the sea ground on the land,
beneath the shadow of a ruined jetty, as we drove away.

At My Mother's Funeral

In memory of Mary Stanley (1919–1980) and Molly MacAlister (1920–1979)

I remember a clear lake with birds
and, inside the chapel, birds, too.
They flew, bronze in sunlight
streaming through the roof, above
the plinth where the casket rested.
Two women whom I loved were dead
and it seemed right they should be
together there in death.
                       As religion assures us
the soul leaves the body in death,
so the birds rose up in flight.
It seemed to me that all outdoors
was with us in that tiny room.
A casket is not much space
to hold a body, but what walls can hold
a heart and all the love that it contains?

Last Day With My Brother

for Chris Smithyman (1947–1984)

We carry our deaths with us and yours
was already large within you –
two years in remission, or so they said.
What I remember most of all
was your quality of sad forbearance –
your struggle to come to terms with
the disappointment of your life.
In those last photographs of us together,
you did not, could not smile.
Yet you could smile in life.
We laughed and sang our way
over the Wellington hills that day
in search of a friend with a beach house
out on the coast.

Arriving, there was nobody there.
Just a house, disquietingly empty,
as all houses are, in their owners' absence,
like a garment, waiting to be put on.

We drove away again and, late in the afternoon,
stopped at a fish 'n' chip shop down by the water.
Green estuary water, choppy in a chill easterly wind,
and the warmth of fish 'n' chips in their steaming
newsprint package…

Smiling, we came home
and it was time for me to go.
That last moment, then,
while the taxi stood, door open, waiting –
that last moment as we stood in embrace
(the last embrace this side of the grave, brother)
some small spark of electricity passed between us,
a little bolt, starting somewhere down by the knees
and travelling upwards between our bodies
to separate us with the shock. We both stood back,
embarrassed, laughing, not knowing
what to make of it.

Then I stepped into the taxi
and was gone.

The reason that I write this down is to record
the love there was between us, the terrible,
sad loss our bodies knew much sooner
than our minds

and to say, one last time this side of the grave, brother,

Hail and farewell.

The Smell of Coffee

When I was young, I used to be sent to the corner grocery store to purchase fresh coffee for Mother and Father. At the store, I would push my money across the counter and the grocer, a Wingate's Chindits' veteran (he drank), would grind the beans loudly in the shiny, red machine, then push a brown paper bag, full of the freshly ground coffee, shakily back to me. I would walk out of the shop with my nose pressed hard against the top of the bag, where I kept it all the way home. I loved that rich, dark smell, redolent of jungles and adventure – a smell which dominated my childhood. Mother and Father boiled the coffee in a pot on the back of the stove, then drank it, black, hot and strong, as fuel for their interminable war.

Memories of Nile Road and Wairau Creek

Nile Road…the house on the side of the hill…
The ramparts round the top proclaimed
its true nature. It was a house designed
for fighting. Its flat cement roof could hardly
contain my parents' anger. Not that we boys
noticed. We were too busy, playing in the dirt
under the house, among the orchard trees,
or down the bottom of the garden, by the creek,
which was still fit for play, in those days.
We fished for eels, caught tadpoles in pools,
made miniature canoes from flax wood
and raced them downstream. With other boys,
we paddled corrugated iron punts as far
as the willow swamp, where we took part
in wars with slingshots, stones, and homemade
bows and arrows – a miracle how no one
lost an eye! Within a few years we couldn't play
in the creek anymore. Neighbourhood sewage
drained into it, choking its dark brown water
with bright green slime. Then a paint factory
further up the valley emptied arsenic into it
and all the eels crawled out on its banks to die,
stomachs exploding, stinking in the summer heat.

After that, the creek became a place of sadness,
somewhere to be shunned, like the house
on the side of the hill. We boys grew up
and moved away. Our parents were still fighting –
night and day, their rancorous voices never stopped.
Constant abuse, screams and recriminations poisoned
the air. Childhood was over, but we were to find
we took that failure, that despair, with us everywhere.

Learning to Fall

for Gerard Smithyman

At Ohinewai, we parked the car down by the sea,
where the creek crossed the road, and walked
through a stony, thistle-strewn paddock
to the little groin of bush at the base of the hills.
There, a waterfall fell down the hill in steps –
each step a bowl, emptying itself into the next,
until they filled a deep pool at the bottom.
In the shady clearing, we took off all our clothes
and climbed buck-naked up the steep hillside,
past the cairn of stones which held a human skull
and thighbone – ancient guardians of the spot –
and out onto a high, dome-shaped rock, not unlike
a skull itself. In death's cold eye we leapt and hung
in space a moment, suspended. In that moment,
it seemed, with all of space before us and the past behind –
the sad, useless baggage of our lives discarded
along with our clothes – we were suddenly, absurdly free.

Bowling Green

Every autumn this disruption,
this violence. The lawn, immaculate,
is scalped, skinned, taken back
to the bone, the geometry beneath,
a simple square of underlying dirt
and clay. Worse still, it is turned up,
routered, rotary-hoed, until its surface,
once serene, becomes a battleground,
a place of death and resurrection.
Oh these seasonal transformations!
Birth and death and death and birth…
Each spring they bring the rollers out
and roll it flat and smooth
as a polished ballroom floor, then sow
a miniature forest of green spears,
sharp as desire, sweet
as the memory of love.
Summer brings out the men in white –
the unexpected purity of their costumes
against clipped grass – cigarettes
in mouths, big stomachs hanging,
swinging the bowls in wide arcs
towards the jack, dreaming
of that beer over lunch. And so
another summer passes, with puffed clouds
over the downtown towers riding,
like sailboats on the lake…

Waiting for the Penguins

'Catch that wave!' – old '60s saying

Here we are,
sitting on cold, concrete bleachers
under blazing arc-lights
and the hard eyes of security guards,
surrounded by rich Americans
wearing Akubra hats, Drizabones
and RM Williams boots, waiting
for the penguins.
A bone-chilling wind
blows off the sea.
My wife and daughter
sit beside me, shivering
under blankets. Only my young son
will not sit still.
He runs around, antic spirit,
up and down the bleachers
and out onto the beach
where we are not allowed to go,
and has to be retrieved.

Somewhere out in the darkness
a furry flotilla is gathering,
riding the backs
of the deep ocean swells,
turning tiny beaks
slowly towards the shore.
The penguins arrive
in ones and twos and threes.
Unconscious comedians, they stagger
and dither in the surf,
like miniature, drunken Charlie Chaplins,
amid the flare and dazzle
of forbidden flashbulbs.
But they make it onto the beach –
brave little balls of fluff –
more and more and more of them,
marching up the daylit strip of sand,
a comic opera army of brown dots,
heading to their homes in the dark.

I want to cheer, but do not want
to be thought peculiar
by our American cousins
who are already packing away
their expensive cameras, brushing off
their Drizabones and heading back
to where their tour buses wait.
Instead, I collect my recalcitrant son,
cuddle closer to my wife and daughter
and think about the coldness of the night,
the wildness of the sea,
the frailty of those penguins…
Sometimes I think life's like that,
waiting, far out in the dark,
for a wave to rise
which will carry us to that distant shore
of all our dreams and wishes.

Plenty

Now I am thinking of
fishing in the Gap with my father
when young. Putt-putting out
in my father's best friend's aluminium dinghy
with the two-stroke Johnson on the back
to the channel between
the islands and the mainland
where the fish ran free
at the turning of the tides.
We stopped in green water,
a little stirred up by light winds,
attracted by the circling of the gulls.
We dropped anchor, baited hooks
and sat bobbing, drifting, waiting,
passing the time in idle chatter.

We didn't have to wait long.
First one fish struck, then another
and another, so fast we could hardly
haul them in. Snapper – big snapper, too.
We must have been right over
a whole school of them. All we had to do
was wrestle the hook out
of a fish's mouth, drop it
in the bottom of the boat
where it flipped and flopped
and smashed itself to death against the bulwarks,
bait up, drop the line in again
and haul another one up.
It was a fisherman's dream, unreal, hallucinatory.

We caught forty in a couple of hours between us.
It was a kind of frenzy, a delirium.
We didn't stop until the tide stood still
and the fishing ran out.

Looking back, I wonder
what we did with all those fish.
Ate some, smoked some,
gave some to neighbours…
and the rest?

Later, putt-putting back,
my father and his best friend shared beers
and told tall stories in the stern,
while I stretched out in the bow,
drowsy with seasickness
or the tired glow
of fishing frenzy satisfied –

happiness.

The Road to the Coast

(Rainy Day at Walkerville)

We took that road all afternoon
through pouring rain,
the country green and sodden,
the river in flood.
It led us past cows and sheep,
sheltered under dripping branches,
looking out on a wet world
with the patient, long-suffering eyes
of the perpetually downtrodden.
We passed through towns
that were the merest echoes,
memories of other people's holidays.

At a pub down by the river,
a country wedding was breaking up.
Gusts of music through an open window,
shouts, laughter, the sounds
of car doors slamming…
and one drunken man,
mounted on his bicycle,
went wobbling off
to go fishing with his dog.

But our goal lay elsewhere.
We kept on moving
across low, rolling hills,
their scrub-covered darkness
lightened only
by slashes of yellow clay,
until we came to the coast.

We stood and watched
the great, glassy, dimpled waves
come lumbering in.
We saw yachts going about,
their wet sails flapping
like ghosts in the grey gloom.
We looked towards that other ghost,
the distant promontory,
low down on the horizon
like a bank of darker cloud,
merging sea and sky.

Oh the heart, the heart
has needs of its own, to follow
something as indefinite
as a whisper, a promise
of another shoreline, setting out,
if in imagination only,
across grey water,
misted, pearled by rain…

The Market

for Grant Campbell

Working as a barrow boy in the market,
that's the life!

Up at four
to start work at five.
Racing between loading bay and market floor
with barrow loads of produce
piled perilously high,
the damp earth smells of fruit and vegetables
rich in our nostrils,
sweating in the early morning chill…

Once, two barrow boys started a fight –
the hard, smacking sounds of fists on flesh,
blood and spittle flying through the air,
right in front of us –

until somebody pulled them apart.

Another time, we got a job
cleaning out a cool store full of lemons
which had been left to rot
to keep the price high.
All morning, we crouched in that cool-store,
surrounded by the smell of lemons,
freshly zesty or sickly sweet,
turning to mush and mould…

sorting out the good lemons from the bad.

Six Poems Based on Paintings by Edward Hopper

1 House at Dusk

People actually live in these rooms.
See them at twilight,
sewing, talking, just walking around.
Someone has turned a light on,
answering the streetlight outside.
They have lives of their own
that do not matter to us.
We have our own lives, too.
At dusk we are observers.
The trees gather darkly behind the house
in a solid wall.
The long, yellow, end-of-evening sky
stretches to grey clouds
at the horizon, fading
like the last notes
of Roland's horn,
like the call of the infinite,
ridiculously sublime.

2 Night Windows

From my window
I can see
night windows
lit up in the dark –
someone's bedroom,
green carpet,
brown bed,
a radiator on the wall
and a woman bending over
in a red slip,
the shape of her buttocks
firmly outlined
in light and shade
(those most private parts, of course,
most darkly, most discreetly shaded)
while opposite,
a curtain, blowing out
in the night breeze –

desire set free.

3 New York Movie

The lovers kiss.
The music swells
towards its climax.
Soon the end credits will roll,
the audience will leave

satisfied.

Underneath the soft exit light,
the usher is dreaming, dreaming…

And does she dream of love?
No, she is tired,
her feet hurt,
she has seen this movie
too many times before.
She dreams of home,
of being able to sit down, at last,
of dinner.

Tonight, perhaps, of all nights,
somebody else will make her

dinner.

She is tired,
she is hungry.
She dreams of home.
She wishes the movie
were already over.

4 Sunlight in the Cafeteria

The subject is always sunlight.

What happens
when two people meet?
They say hullo,
they don't say hullo,
they have a cup of coffee together
(maybe they don't),
they share a meal,
they spend the rest
of their lives together,

they never see each other again.

What does it matter to us,
who are only onlookers?

The woman looks down,
looks coy – she could
be interested. The man
gestures towards her,
but could be thinking
of something else.

He could just be smoking his cigarette.

Neither of them
has got their coffee yet.

Neither of them
is particularly attractive,
for that matter.

But what would people say
about you and me,
if they saw us together?

The streetscape outside
is massive, monochrome –
a granite cliff.

The conditions
are hardly conducive
to romance.

Will love survive
in the big city?

It has about as much chance
as the extraordinarily ugly plant
in the extraordinarily ugly pot
on the windowsill.

Nevertheless, I want it to
(and I know you do, too) –
sentimentalists that we are, both.

Nevertheless, there is
the sunlight on the wall.

Everything else passes.

5 A Woman in the Sun

One day,
you will take all your clothes off
and stand naked
in the rectangle of sunlight
on your bedroom floor.
You will smoke a cigarette calmly,
while you wait.
The sun will warm your body –
belly, breast and thigh –
like an old lover,
like the warmed over coals of love.
You will not be moved.
The same sun that brushes
the side of the green hill
outside the window,
will soon brush the side
of the whole turning world.
You will not turn away from it
now or ever – you will
simply wait. For now,
it is enough.

6 Rooms by the Sea

One day the room will be empty.
One day the sea will come
right to your door.
The afternoon sun,
sliding across the wall,
reminds you
that, in the end,
death will come
very gently, like stepping out
into the next room,
like stepping into the ocean…

like taking the invitation
of that open door.

Swimming in the Mediterranean

'Come in!'
I called to my kids,
climbing down the rusty iron ladder,
bolted to the side of the rocks,
'It's not cold.'
Of course, I lied.
It was freezing.
The water was grassy green
and clear as a pane of glass.
I could see ten or fifteen feet down,
straight to the bottom.
I let go of the ladder
and pushed off
into open water.
The sky was china blue –
the intense, pale blue
of early spring.
I stared into
its cloudless depths
past the fortress
on its mountain headland,
looming darkly over the town.
Nobody joined me
and my body was turning to
a block of ice,
but I didn't mind.

For a brief, delirious moment,
I was alone,
I was free
in those waters of origin,
criss-crossed through centuries
by Greeks, by Romans,
Knights Templar, Turks and Venetians,
crossed now by rust-bucket tankers,
overcrowded ferries, millionaires' yachts
and cruise ships
like floating palaces.
At once incredibly ancient
and eternally young,
how did it remain
so impossibly pure?
I was realising
a lifetime dream;
I was swimming
in the Mediterranean.

Interior at Petworth

Sunlight riots into the room,
Sets everything ablaze,
Dissolving space and banishing gloom
In a glorious, golden haze.

Nothing has strength or solidity,
Outlines blur and substance fades;
No definition there or quiddity,
Nothing coheres as light invades.

Light is the beginning and the end,
The point to which our journeys tend,
And Turner, dying, did not think it odd
To say at the last, 'The sun is God.'

A Walk on Hampstead Heath

Hampstead Heath is wet.
The ground underfoot is muddy.
We walk forest paths –
a wild place in the middle of London!
I think about T.S. Eliot's 'grimpen' –
the kind of word
only Eliot would know.
Lightning has struck a tree trunk,
shattering it.
We come out into a green space
in front of Kenwood,
like a bridesmaid's tiara
on top of the hill.
Inside, Vermeer's girl
plays her guitar in perfect,
diamond-pointed light and Rembrandt's
lined, old face looks at one
as if to say 'I have survived.
(And look what I can do!)'
His hand is a triumphant slash of paint.
Two semicircles in the background
hint at eternity.
We walk home through
West Hampstead and Camden Town,
stopping only outside Keats' house
in the pouring rain to think about
him and Fanny – impossible love
and happiness so far off…

At Haworth

After inspecting
the family dolls' house,
the tiny couch
where Emily died,
the even tinier dresses
she and her sisters wore,
we walked outside
into the moss-covered graveyard,
overshadowed by
tall, skinny elms
where rooks nested
with their raucous cries,
checked out the family memorial
in the cold, stone church,
and drank in a succession
of local pubs,
each lower, darker and smokier
than the other, each
with its own chair
at the fireside where
poor Bramwell sat, before,
drunk, opiated, he trudged
his slow way back
up the gloomy hillside
to share his father's bed.

Later, we tried to walk
out of the graveyard
onto winter-blackened paddocks,
but could not, because
of foot and mouth restrictions.
So we took the kids and the hired car
and drove out of town –
the end of the line, it seemed,
(or so it was in Emily's time) –
along a narrow, winding road
in search of the famous house.
We never found it, just
a narrower, ever more winding road
and those oddly rounded,
bare, bleak hills, a void,
waiting to be filled
with human feeling,
the passionate heart
which dreams in isolation.

At Castle Howard

That afternoon we arrived late – too late
for admittance – but failed to heed
the head gardener's suggestion we return
some other time. Instead, we walked
around the front lawn, admiring the great
Baroque pile of the house and the view
of its private wood, lake and immense tract
of surrounding countryside – no other
house in sight – while the kids fed a pony
they found in a small enclosure down
by the lake. We walked to the back of the house,
where we admired the formal garden,
with its fountain sculpture of Atlas, holding
the globe up, all by himself, another
immense, empty tract of surrounding country
and the slope, awash with daffodils, leading
to the Temple of the Four Winds, while the kids
chased peacocks between hedgerows.
The sun set and the evening air was freezing,
so we turned to go, but not before we saw
one tired peacock make its heavy-tailed way
up the steps to the great French windows
of the Garden Hall to stand in lonely splendour –
that perfect image of the aristocracy –
lost in contemplation of its reflection in the glass.

Cutting the Grass

Cutting the grass around the house –
the surrounding countryside as green
as Ireland, green as an act of faith,
before the summer heat. Remembering
the first time we came here, following
the real estate agent in a high-speed chase
along the narrow country roads – I
could hardly believe we would survive.
Arriving at the paddock, we parked
inside the gate, waded through thigh-high grass
to the far end, where the sun was setting
in a blaze of sparks like a Catherine wheel
over Ben Cruachain, disappearing in the haze…
standing on that uneven ground, I felt
like falling to my knees in prayer, eyes
opened to the wonder of the natural world,
like we were stumbling into Paradise.

Briagolong Sundays

Nothing much happens
in Briagolong on Sundays.
A cluster of cars
outside the church
proclaims the true believers.
Everyone else is in bed.
The sunlit streets are silent –
not so much as a child, or a dog, stirs.
The church stares out
across an empty paddock
to the mountains.
The work of man
confronts the world of nature.
Time confronts eternity.
God is absent, or withdrawn,
as the people from the town.
The church itself will surely pass,
like the frail bell tower set next
to it, teetering on skeletal iron legs.
In the end, there will
only be the mountains –
in winter, with snow on the ridges,
in summer, dissolving in the heat.

Wattle in Winter

I'm not the kind of man, you understand,
who habitually cuts flowers and arranges them
in vases, yet here I am, in the depths of winter,
picking my way gingerly across wet grass
to the wattle tree at the far end of the property,
to cut a fluffy cloud of golden wattle blossom
and carry it back inside the house like a shining prize,
a trophy. There I trim it, tailor it, position it carefully
in the vase to what, I hope, is maximum effect,
its blaze of yellow set startlingly against a backdrop
of iridescent blue Pride of Madeira spears. I stand
and admire my handiwork. Now I am happy;
now I am satisfied. In the middle of winter, I have
the promise of summer; I have the sun inside my house.

A Perfect Night For Shooting Stars

'A perfect night for shooting stars…'
was what we said when we pulled up
at the front door and stepped out
under the glittering dome of night.
The air was frosty and the breath
rose from our mouths like Puffing Billy,
labouring up a slope. The sky
was perfectly clear, with an intensity
of black deepening on blackness
that gave a dizzying sense of infinite space.
There were stars behind the stars –
look, the Milky Way spread its cloudy stain
across the centre of the sky, as we
craned our necks to see! But it was late,
you were tired, so we unpacked, went inside,
had drinks, you went to bed and it wasn't
till much later that I stepped outside again,
drink in hand, for one last glimpse of
those dazzling stars. I looked up to where
the peak of the roof cut an upside-down
black V against the glimmering light
of the galaxy and saw a golden shooting star
trace a sudden path across the height
of that shining night.

                    It was so perfect,
I almost failed to believe it, almost forgot
to make a wish – but then, I wondered,
what should I wish for? Should I wish
for gold? It seemed appropriate, but
somehow I could not. Then I thought about
the beauty of that night, the warmth
of your body, lying in our bed, the dregs
of whisky, swirling in my glass, and I wished –
foolishly perhaps – for happiness that lasts.
If you have happiness, I reasoned, you have
the best that people long for when they wish
for all the rest – money, fame, success –
whatever it is that fills their dreams.
Or so it seemed to me, as I turned and went
back inside to where you lay, knowing
I should not tell my wishes, to you or anyone,
if I wanted them to come true at the end
of this, or any other, long and tiring day.

The World is a Garden

for Joy Dunstan

I watch you move between the trees at sunset,
against a backdrop of those mountains,
disappearing into night. You hold the leaves
tenderly in your hand, checking them,
as you once held the fingers of your children,
coming in from the garden with a scratch or bruise,
before administering the healing benison
of kiss and Band-Aid. I am reminded of
other gardens you have made, transforming
backyards into wonderlands where even adults
would lose themselves in childlike delight.
Somehow, you were always planting, fork
or spade in hand, sowing seeds, burying the roots
of trees in earth, then standing devotedly
for hours on end, with hose and contemplative
glass of wine, watering them in. You seemed
to have an innate understanding, a deep,
instinctual sympathy for the quaternity
of seed, soil, sun and rain that answered to
imperatives of growth within. Yours was a life
of constant nurture, raising plants,
as you raised our children. Those gardens,
like our children, are grown now, passed on
to other hands and other lives, and here you are,
starting on your latest garden, your largest yet –
a country paddock, so far removed from the city
it could be the far side of that rising moon – but
in changing times and difficult conditions,

with a climate that can no longer be relied on,
that brings us constant drought and heatwaves,
impossible high winds and devastating fires. Almost
enough to make you despair, except I know you will not.
I bring you out another glass of wine. Together,
we toast the sunset. The world is a garden. Care for it.

Briagolong Mornings

First the birds – the carolling magpies,
the squawking cockatoos and twittering wrens –
then the light around the edges of the blind,
like a bright frame around a picture of darkness,
tenebrous, profound. Rising for my early morning pee,
I pull the blind half up. The landscape rushes in –
the end of our paddock, with its dilapidated fence,
shored up against ruin, the meandering path
the neighbour's cows walk, returned from milking,
the riverflat paddocks below, covered with maize,
like the green baize of a billiards table, the line of trees
along the creek and, further off, the mountains,
swimming into view, the morning mist lifting
to reveal their primordial bulk, before
the haze of the day settles in. So day begins
at Briagolong and is repeated again and again,
in bright sunshine, overcast and rain, snow
on the ridges in winter and smoke in summer,
until the end of time, if that day comes –
the original miracle, light out of darkness,
sun coming up and moon going down, night dying
and day being born. I have my pee, make coffee
and bring it into the bedroom, but already
the morning is older, has lost its glow.
Impossible to believe now that first, trembling promise,
as the day looms, with all its obligations, its commitment
to the absolutely ordinary which constitutes our lives.

The Last of the Season

Autumn, and we have the small pool at the Quarry
to ourselves. We lie out on the gravel beach,
so finely ground, it might almost be sand.
Dragonflies and swimmer bugs strike coruscating light,
landing on the surface of the water. The birds
are oddly silent, as if they have abandoned the bush,
along with the tourists. After the rain, the water
is astonishingly clear, a condensed continuation,
somehow, of the air. We immerse ourselves in it
gently, a bit at a time, lying in the warm shallows,
then slipping slowly out into the colder depths.
At length, we are afloat, moving our arms and legs
like those same swimmer bugs, while the last
currents of summer carry us downstream like leaves.

Black Snake on the Road

Driving between Bushy Park
and Briagolong – a long,
straight stretch of road, heat haze
shimmering off the surface
like water, making it hard to see
what lay ahead – there was
a sudden movement there,
a blurring, a shaking,
something not quite right
in the middle of the road,
an unreadable shadow,
a blacker shade of black, against
the boiling bitumen.

We looked again and saw
it was no shadow but
a large black snake, hit
by a passing car or truck,
writhing there in its
death agony, flailing
and lashing like a whip.
We came upon it
too fast, too suddenly,
for us to brake and avoid it;
we simply had to pass
right over the top
and pray that somehow
we had missed it, that we
had not provided it
with any dark opportunity

to wrap itself around our axle
and climb, undetected,
into the comfort and security
of our air-conditioned cabin.
                        Such overwhelming panic!
Our minds were plunged into a blackness
like guilt we cannot be rid of, or
our fear of death itself, which
follows us like a rumour,
an insidious suggestion, threatening
to undermine us, to envelope us
even in the middle
of the clearest, blue day.

Imagine our relief
when we looked back to see
that same agonised writhing in
our rear-view mirror. Not us
and not this time, we thought (no inkling of
sweet *Schadenfreude* here!). Together,
we exhaled our pent up breath; I gripped
the wheel with a new resolve
and we drove nervously, gratefully on.

Goanna in the Grass

'Did you see that?' I asked, pulling up
in a shower of stones and dust
at the roadside. 'Yes,' you nodded,
as we both stared behind us
at what we had seen – a goanna,
the size of a grown man, standing,
stock-still, at the bottom of a grassy hill, like
a statue from some antediluvian time,
staring fixedly at the farmhouse
on top of the hill.
                       White, the farmhouse,
and dark, the goanna, like polished bronze,
its legs astride a torso the thickness
and muscularity of a wrestler's, with something
of a wrestler's arrogance, too,
in the way it held its head up high,
this relic of an ancient time,
ruler over the landscape it surveyed. It seemed,
in the arrogance of the way it stood,
to pose a challenge to the order
we humans like to think we have made.

We backed up fast, to take a closer look,
but, by the time we got there, it had vanished,
trackless, in the long summer grass,
and we were left to struggle with our disbelief,
and something else – a sense of loss,
of shame, even, at the way
we have banished such creatures to the sidelines,
the margins of life, and, in doing that,
sadly limited our own chances of encountering
the extraordinary in the ordinary one day,
standing quite casually at the roadside, as if
it had never been away…

Four Birds

What is it about birds? They bring
a greater perspective with them,
like those cockatoos that tumble round the sky
on silver, glistening wings, screeching
delight and hostility at each other – or anybody
else who's prepared to listen –
their comic, intense satisfaction in
the momentary excitement of being alive.
Then, sailing through, like an invasion
from an alien universe, their antimatter,
their shadowy counterpart, their mysterious,
dark cousins, the black cockatoos, which
are silent and discreet as they (the white cockatoos)
are rowdy and ridiculous.
                        Or those rosellas, sweetening
the thorn bush, the unbelievable redness
of their breasts glowing like traffic lights at dusk –
a colour which is all radiance and has
no precise limits. And finally – majestic visitation –
those two wedge-tailed eagles which flew low
over the paddock, late one afternoon, to settle
on the gum trees by the gate for a moment
in lonely condescension before spreading
their immense black-tipped wingspans
and taking off again, sublimely indifferent
to the awe they created in their wake.
They remind us of who we are and what we lack,
we who can only look and long, but never
roar so wholly, gratifyingly with laughter,
mystify, blaze or soar above the world like them.

Hare

We see you every time we arrive
At the property, standing to attention,
Nose to the wind, finely tuned
For danger – then the nervous scamper
To your bolt-hole in the grass.

We do not mean to disturb you
And sometimes, indeed, we feel
Almost apologetic about our intrusion
Into what has quite clearly, in
Our absence, become your domain.

Or we see you in the morning,
Hopping to inspect us, sometimes
Coming right up to the house.
When you hear us moving, you freeze
Like a statue, like that other hare,

Drawn by Dürer, every piece of fur
And whisker, every fleshy fold
Of ear and nostril, each flashing eye
Quiveringly alive. Sometimes I think
I should shoot you and have visions of you,

Bubbling in the pot. But, on the whole,
I think not. You have done no harm
That we can see so far and, to your credit,
You keep us in touch with that wild nature
The steady spread of houses from the town

Does its best to suppress. So here's to you,
Guardian of the paddock, our unwitting friend,
With whom we, however temporarily,
Share our lives, before we each come to
Whatever may be, in time, our individual ends.

Giant Swing

Some things in life are inevitable.
So the others, pulling on the rope,
raise you slowly up to the top of the pole.
There is no help, and no view, from here.
Cut off inside your helmet, you are
islanded, cocooned, aware only
of what is immediately in front of you.
The voices of the others come distantly to you,
chanting 'One, two, three…'
                              You pull
the red release cord. There is
a moment's silence, stillness.
You drop down with a jolt.
Then a giant force takes hold of you,
hurls you backwards through twin poles
at the far end of the swing, like they are
football posts and you are the ball.
The next thing you are aware of
is being suspended, sixty feet
above the ground, looking down
at the upturned faces of the others below,
sprinkled like daisies in a field.
This must be what trapeze artists feel like,
or gymnasts, as they fly through the air
like reckless birds. Then you are off again
like 'a skate's heel', as Manley Hopkins says,
while you hang on desperately to your
frail piece of rope and pray for
your wild ride to end.

                    Afterwards,
there is relief, a shaky calm, an uncanny feeling
of having been reborn. Surely, the faint wind
at ground level has never kissed your cheek
so tenderly. There is new energy, new wonder
in your step, as if you have faced the world's dangers
and survived. But always, in your mind,
you are back in position at the top of the arc,
waiting, once again, for that tremendous force to come
and seize you, hurl you, willy nilly, into being.

That Valley, That Shadow

We were driving outside Canberra,
up a long, narrow valley,
off the main road.
We had been driving all afternoon.
I had a lump on my arm
the size of a golf ball.
In the movie in my mind,
we were gangsters on the run
from the police, or lovers
from a jealous husband.
We fled up that valley, trying
to outrun distance, trying
to outrun remoteness, trying
to outrun death itself, until
the road turned into a farm track,
the sky clouded over
and the bush closed in on us,
like a wall. We didn't know
where we were going; we wanted
to turn around and go back,
but there wasn't room. We slowed
to a crawl, like babes, lost in the wood,
thinking we were near the end,
as the darkness grew around us.
Then we saw, ahead of us,
the road widen, gravel-covered once again,
then tar-sealed, and, before we knew it,
we were in Canberra, with
the lights coming on in the dusk.

Interrupted Journeys

Reading a collection of essays, I am reminded suddenly
of my father's story about his father seizing on a leaf
from Table Mountain, Cape Town, found in a book,
and holding it for hours, lost in reverie. Cape Town
was a place he had seen beauty, a place he loved,
a place, implicitly, where he felt he belonged, before
he continued his life's journey, to end, eventually,
in New Zealand and meeting with my grandmother,
which led, in turn, to the birth of my father.
                              The moral here
is clear – no journey, no father (with all its implications
for the present writer). And yet, my grandfather's heart
remained, it seems, stubbornly in love with another time,
another place, a possibility glimpsed, then lost sight of,
to the end of his days. Why is this of interest to me?
It reminds me that I was on a journey when I arrived
in Melbourne, February 1980, forty degrees, a north wind
blowing (something, coming from temperate New Zealand,
I had never experienced – let alone imagined). Melbourne
was going to be a temporary resting place, a pause
on my own, continuing journey to Canada. But then,
of course, a whole lot of other things happened, as they do –
love, work, family, the rest of my life – and somehow
I never completed that journey. I stayed at my temporary
stopping point, while dreaming wistfully, from time to time,
of my intended destination.

It might be objected
that my grandfather had actually been there, where
his heart desired, but the meaning I take is the same,
that all lives are, in some sense, interrupted journeys,
that we are always in progress to do something else
when our lives actually happen, that we live somehow
with a milder version of the exile's despair, a dream
of another life somewhere – an entirely unjustified
nostalgia for what might have been – grateful as we are
for what really did occur. And so it continues, our journey
in the place to which we have become accustomed, surrounded
by the faces with which we have become familiar (which,
with any luck, we love) until we meet our ultimate interruption,
or, perhaps, our final destination. But, of that happy event,
or disaster, until its time comes, let us speak no further.

Mother's Day

Mother's Day in Melbourne was a metaphor for life –
at least, in terms of the weather. One minute,
the sky was all clouded over with pouring rain,
the next, the sky cleared with brilliant sunshine.
The whole family was there, inside the house,
one warm, beating heart, once again, looking out
at that freezing, freakishly changeable weather.
We ate a lavish lunch, drank sparkling wine and talked.
Later, we dropped the children off (children no more)
at their various shared houses across town – Royal Parade,
a blaze of yellow, with the elm trees changing in the cold –
winter not yet on us, autumn not quite gone. All day,
you wore my mother's mother-of-pearl butterfly brooch,
pinned at your throat, old lady style. I thought
of a woman whom neither you nor the children knew,
and I thought how that brooch would one day fly
from you to our daughter, and so on down the years,
a cherished heirloom and a diminishing memory.

Wet Winter

Winter in Melbourne is grey – it rains all day, all night,
with a cold that seeps into the bones. The reservoirs
are nearly full, which fills everybody with hope – these
are the fat years after the lean. If only we could enjoy them.
The stock market rises and falls faster than a speeding car.
Every day we are riveted to its roller-coaster ride
and the sad fate of our diminishing superannuation.
Workers are laid off, companies rationalise, the right wing
sees its opportunity. While politicians posture and seek
to manipulate the masses, we forget the poor old earth,
which should be the focus of our attention. She sleeps fitfully,
like an old dog, neglected in a corner, but has a knack
of reminding those who overlook her, at their peril.
In those same mountains where the storm waters gather,
the spring growth waits, which a single spark will ignite
into a summer inferno. I fear that moment when La Nina
turns to El Niño and hear, already, the chorus of voices
'We should have taken more care of this!' The old earth
shudders and turns in her sleep. From winter's conflicted
complacency, I look forward to the summer with dread.

Washington Square Blues

By Washington Square fountain I sat down and wept
with sheer tiredness after walking the streets
of Greenwich Village all afternoon. Washington Square! –
where black dudes call out and challenge you
to a game of chess, as you pass, students play frisbee
on the grass, lie around in groups, talking,
or read alone. The ghosts of demonstrations past punch
the air or chant collectively, in my imagination,
under a cloudless sky. We walk to Tompkins Square
for a drink at McSorley's saloon, only to find it
filled by a reunion of Afghanistan veterans – huge men
in military uniforms and biker patches, spilling
out into the street, their Harleys parked like a barricade
against outside interference. We leave them
to their beer and their memories and sit in the square
with the bums and the junkies to regroup
for our journey home. The sign on the Village Voice
building behind us fades like a far-off echo
of Vietnam moratoria and politically more active days.

At the Hotel Chelsea

closed for renovation, 2012

I stood in the lobby and breathed its heady air of decay
and immortality. The desk clerk treated me with glacial disdain,
warming slightly to hand me a pamphlet on the renovation.
I saw workmen in the next room participating in that great New York
tradition of tearing down the old to make way for the new.
I dreamed of those secret, forbidden depths – of Dylan, lying in bed,
a sick junkie, writing 'Sad Eyed Lady of The Lowlands'
for his future wife, or that other Dylan (the former's namesake) –
as it said on the plaque outside – 'sailing' out of there 'to die.'
It was a kind of heaven and a hell, too, for those who chose to live there –
the license of total freedom and the guarantee of absolute privacy,
like some inverted, secular temple of the arts – or even for travellers
like me, disappointed or not, who were only passing through.

Wall Street

There is trouble in the heart of the economy –
trouble in the heart of the country. On Wall Street,
the country's cashbox is wrapped in the American flag
like somebody's going away present, but it fails
to deliver the necessary strength, the necessary
confidence in the system that overtook the world.
On Sunday, the suits are missing, but the messages
from the avenues (and laneways) of power around it
are the same. New York, they seem to say, was the city
of the twentieth century, but, somewhere in Asia,
the city of the twenty-first century is building.
Uncomfortably close to Ground Zero, even though
the towers are being rebuilt, it is hard to believe
America's time has not come and gone. Outside
Federal Hall, the statue of George Washington
stands with heartfelt pride – pride in achievement,
pride in the tradition those early patriots created,
carried on by the immigrants – tired, poor and teeming –
who built a new, democratised Europe, on this side
of the Atlantic, far surpassing the old. But even
the doughty farmer, standing in front of Federal Hall's
neo-classical façade (the very place he was inaugurated),
does not look entirely convinced that glory can survive.

Brooklyn Bridge

So, Walt Whitman, you imagined me,
crossing Brooklyn Bridge on a warm
and sunny day of early autumn –

and I thought that I saw you with
a big straw hat, cherubic face and
curly hair and beard. But, perhaps

I was mistaken. Certainly, you were
not among the girls who jumped up
on the barrier and struck fashion poses

for each other to photograph against
the Lower Manhattan skyline. Neither
were you with the man who carried

his poodle all the way across and back.
But your spirit was there, in the mighty
crowd that flowed one way, then

the other – men, women, children,
cyclists, dogs – who all contributed
to the party, one giant celebration

of technology and democracy, of which
you, Walt Whitman, would most heartily
have approved. Hard, too, to ignore

the upsweep of those cables, as Stella
depicted them, a secular cathedral,
a hymn to progress, on their way

to Hart Crane's God. And I walked
with the crowd, overtaking and being
overtaken, stepping sideways to avoid

the mad onrush of cyclists with
their urgently shrilling bells. I walked
from Manhattan to the Brooklyn end,

stopping just long enough to feel
that I stood on foreign soil, before
returning. Traffic roared beneath

the boardwalk, pleasure craft cut
white wakes across the blue river
out towards Liberty and the Island.

Returning, Gehry's Beekman Building
dominated the view, rippling like
a flag unfurled, or more ominously,

an anti-structure melting, dissolving
to its base, in an ambiguous gesture
towards the new World Trade towers

rising from Ground Zero behind it.

Storm in Boston

A storm is building in Boston.
All day, gusts of wind
and splashes of rain
prefigure its coming. We walk

to Boston Common, stopping
to photograph McCloskey's ducks
and Saint-Gauden's Civil War memorial.
The gold dome of the statehouse gleams

with self-congratulatory pride.
A black Freedom Walk guide
extols the prescient virtues
of the state constitution. Lowell knew

the conquest of space was nearer
than peace and equality between people.
The bums asleep in the park
preserve their indifference. The wind

gusts harder over Beacon Hill,
the Charles River and the Harvard Yard.
By the time we return to our guest house,
the sky is darkening and the rain is nearer.

The wind whines around the corners
of the ageing brownstone,
tearing leaves and bits of broken branch
off the trees. But this is Boston.

The flood Lowell feared
will not wash anything away. Nevertheless,
it will come – and come tonight –
in a storm, raging across Boston and the bay.

Return to Melbourne

Bell Street looks small and suburban,
the traffic surprisingly sparse, returned
from the centre to the periphery.
The rest of the world looks very far away.
America becomes something, once more,
we watch on TV – those distant figures
of wealth and power who determine
the fate of the world.
                    Leaving New York,
Forty-Second Street is cleared all the way
down to the UN. Obama is in town, the taxi
driver explains. We crane our necks, looking
up and down that vast, empty boulevard,
but see nothing of importance, only a few,
bored cops, waiting in their cars.

                              The rigours
of the flight consume us. We survive, if only
marginally, to be ejected at the other end
into quite another place and time.
Melbourne awaits us, flat and sprawling,
with something of the disappointment
of the ordinary, a contempt for the familiar,
the too well-known. At the same time,
it reaches out to embrace us. The return
to family and friends – how would
we survive without them? This is what
we survive for – the triumph of the quotidian,
which we sink back into as into the welcome
comfort of our own bed. It may not be exotic,
it may not bulge with wealth and power,
upside down at the bottom of the world…

but it is home.

In Praise of Nectarines

All life's grandeur
Is something with a girl in summer…
                'Waking Early Sunday Morning', Robert Lowell

Supreme pleasure of the summer,
my favourite fruit, the nectarine…
The tree in the backyard yields its few treasures
after this wet summer of high winds, heavy rains
and hail. As always, they are worth waiting for –
the intensity only increased by the scarcity –
the warmth of the few, true summer days
preserved in the soft, white, rounded flesh,
the explosion of sweet juice in the mouth,
followed by the piercing tartness, which gives
that overwhelming sweetness an edge,
a wildness beyond any I have known, except,
perhaps, the first, heady days of a new love,
clung to with such hope and fear, when young.

In Memory of George Haydn, 1919–2005

Brother, when you describe a 'small world' encounter
with a childhood friend of George's, I am reminded
of meeting George myself, for the first time in many years,
at our father's funeral. I was surprised by how small he was,
or had become, shrunk with age, and how he held my hand
through the ceremony, looking after the distraught adult
as he had once looked after the teenage escapee
from the warring house. Or was I holding his hand, as he mourned
the passing of his generation, feeling the time come closer
when he would take his own walk to the edge of space
and let the winds that blow before and after time bear him away?

An Old Dog's Tale

Dust in sunlight and memory in corners
'A Song for Simeon', T.S. Eliot

We are living with an old dog,
who sleeps most of the day and night,
waking only to lurch, on arthritic legs,
vaguely in the direction of food bowl
or the great outdoors. Deaf and blind,
he bumps into furniture, walks
head on into walls, jams himself
in corners, or spends whole minutes
at a time in apparent contemplation
of some mysterious essence of life
we cannot perceive. Amusing, pitiable,
perhaps, and certainly frustrating,
when he will not get out from underfoot,
he follows us around, in search
of food, of contact, a little companionship
in these latter days of his journey.
Tempting to see an image of ourselves
there, too, grown old and feeble,
doddering on shaky pins towards
a future we are never going to remember…

Extinction looms for all of us, but,
for him, sooner rather than later.
Therefore, we pamper him, make him
as comfortable as we can, excuse
the occasional lapse of his bladder,
or worse, and count each day
he is with us a very small blessing,
as we all make our way through
our too short pilgrimage on planet Earth.

www.ingramcontent.com/pod-product-compliance
Lightning Source LLC
Chambersburg PA
CBHW062151100526
44589CB00014B/1779